W9-ARO-360

promise of a new spring

the holocaust and renewal

by
GERDA WEISSMANN KLEIN

Illustrated by
VINCENT TARTARO

PHOENIX FOLIOS
Scottsdale, Arizona

Books by Gerda Weissmann Klein
ALL BUT MY LIFE
THE BLUE ROSE
A PASSION FOR SHARING
PEREGRINATIONS

Library of Congress Cataloging in Publication Data

Klein, Gerda Weissmann, 1924–
  Promise of a new spring

  1. Holocaust, Jewish (1939–1945)—Juvenile
literature. I. Tartaro, Vincent. II. Title.
D810.J4K57   940.53'15'03924   81–14368
ISBN 0-940646-51-X   AACR2

© Copyright 1981 by Gerda Weissmann Klein
Illustrations © copyright 1981 by Vincent Tartaro

Photo credits: Wide World, pp. 6,7,8,9.
Zionist Archives: p. 5.

Published by
PHOENIX FOLIOS

Manufactured in MEXICO.

This book is dedicated to
Alysa, Julie, Andrew,
Melissa, Lindsay, Jessica,
Jennifer, and Alexa,
and all the inheritors
of a new spring.

G.W.K.

For Diane –

To Life !

Fondly,

Lenore L. ____

A long time ago,
but still within memory of many people
there was a great tragedy, the Holocaust.
Holocaust means destruction and loss of life,
by fire.

An evil man, Hitler—
    and his followers, the Nazis—
rose to power.
    They chose the swastika (a twisted cross) as their sign;
        and they conquered country after country.
    The Nazis wanted to make the free people of the world their slaves.

Good people everywhere fought against the Nazis.
Six long years they fought.
At times it seemed the Nazis might even win.

At last the war was over. The Nazis were defeated.
The countries of Europe were set free.
Free from terror and free from slavery.

But the Nazis left their evil mark behind.
Cities had been destroyed;
    people had lost loved ones.

Those who suffered most
were the Jewish people.
The Nazis took jobs away from the Jews
and kept Jewish children
from going to school.

The Nazis forced the Jews
to wear yellow badges.

The Nazis decided to kill every Jew—
     the young and the old together.
And to destroy every memory
     of the Jewish people, too.
They burned Jewish books.
     Books are ways of remembering,
    but the Nazis wanted the world to forget the Jews.

They forced the Jews to live behind walls,
apart from their old friends and neighbors,
and closed the gates so that
the Jews could not go in or out.

Many Jews were killed in the cities and in the
countryside. But the Nazis sent most Jews to
special places called concentration camps.
Behind the barbed wire fences of the concentration camps,
the Nazis murdered the Jews.

The Nazi murder of the Jews is called the Holocaust.
The Holocaust was as terrible for human beings,
as a forest fire is for nature.

Imagine the world as a forest, with trees and flowers;
a forest filled with many creatures,
much as our own world is.
The seasons are the order of life.

In spring, life is born. Trees grow new leaves, birds hatch from eggs in nests. Bear cubs look out at the world with startled eyes.
Violets bloom by the rushing brook, adding their perfume to the new spring.

Then comes summer.
    Leaves grow darker on the branches,
    the trees are dense and green.
    Young birds have learned to fly;
the young deer, their legs no longer wobbly,
    run through the forest
    to find water at the brook.

After summer the autumn comes.
Now the forest is rich with berries
         and mushrooms, fruits and nuts.
Squirrels gather acorns and nuts,
         hiding them in the hollows of the trees
so they will have food for the winter.
         Birds' nests are empty now.
         The young have flown away.

Finally, snow begins to fall.
Gently, slowly, from darkened skies,
millions of snowflakes like white lacy stars,
silently drift downward.
They are a thick, soft blanket
gently covering the sleeping forest.

Winter, after all, is not death.
It is a long, deep, refreshing sleep, as if nature
were saying: "Hush! Sleep, gather your strength
for the coming spring."
Just as you need to sleep at night to wake up fresh
for the new day, so winter is necessary
for the rebirth of spring.

The flowers did not really die—
only the flowers of one summer withered,
only the flowers of one generation are gone.
From their clumps, from their roots and their seeds,
new flowers, exactly like those that are gone,
will bloom again come spring.

In nests on tree branches
another generation of birds will wake to life
and will raise its many voices in song.
The butterfly's eggs, well protected from the cold,
will hatch as the sunlight gets stronger
and the days are warm again.

That is the cycle of life,
the never-ending chain of life,
going on and on as before!

But what if an evil hand
    decided to set fire to the forest
one spring or summer—
    decided to destroy all life out of season?

The tiny squirrels just looking out at the world,
the eggs in their nests still unhatched,
the flowers just starting to bloom,
the fireflies before they had a chance to glow.
Even the mighty oak tree—
so tall, so strong, so old.

All of them: young and old,
    beautiful and plain,
  wise or simple.
Burned, destroyed, killed, out of season,
  out of the normal order of life.

There would be no roots
from which to grow again,
    no eggs from which to hatch
new young ones—
so much of the forest's life
    would be lost forever.

That is what happened
in the time of the Holocaust.
Only a few were saved.

Only a very few.
They were called survivors.

Just as in a forest fire
      some birds, their wings singed by
         the heat and the flames,
might have managed to fly to freedom.

Perhaps there might be an old tree,
     badly burned but still standing
in the silent forest.
    It might have survived
because its roots were deep enough
     to find water below
      the charred forest floor.

It may be able to live again,
to sprout new leaves
on at least one of its branches.

Some of the deer may have run from
the forest in time to be saved.
Perhaps a few bunnies survived
in a hollow below the earth
—the last few left from a large family.

So are the few human survivors of the Holocaust.
They have an important task now.
To build a new life . . .

To remember what the world was like
    before so much was destroyed by evil.

To repeat their memories;
to tell their story
    to children and to grandchildren.
    To all who will listen.

Listen, listen well to the tale
of what they have seen,
     what they have gone through.

For you are the new spring
in the forest of the world.

GERDA WEISSMANN KLEIN, the author, is herself a survivor of the Holocaust. Every member of her family and most of her friends perished in the concentration camps. At the end of the war, she was rescued in Czechoslovakia, after a 350-mile death march in the winter of 1945. Today, she travels and lectures extensively for a variety of organizations that include the United Jewish Appeal, Bonds for Israel, universities, high schools, motivational groups and interfaith gatherings. She is the author of *All But My Life,* the story of her own suffering and survival, a classic, currently in its 38th edition. *The Blue Rose* is a children's book about a special child which has been translated into numerous languages and adapted as a documentary film in India. The book led to the establishment of "The Blue Rose Foundation," dedicated to the mentally retarded. This was followed by *A Passion for Sharing,* a biography of the New Orleans philanthropist and humanitarian Edith Rosenwald Stern, which won the Valley Forge Freedom Award, and *Peregrinations,* a children's book which depicts an artist's flight of fancy during her travels to Mexico. Mrs. Klein is well-known for her columns and profiles for *The Buffalo News.* Among her numerous public honors are the "Woman of the Year" award, four doctorates of humane letters, an Humanitarian citation, the Award of the Year of the Special Child, the Hannah Solomon Award of the National Council of Jewish Women, and the Adele Rosenwald Levy Award of UJA's Women's Division. More recently, the documentary, *One Survivor Remembers,* in which she gives an account of her wartime years, garnered an Emmy Award, a Cable Ace Award, and an Academy "Oscar." Mrs. Klein has two daughters, a son, and eight grandchildren.

VINCENT TARTARO, the artist, was a designer and illustrator whose work has appeared in several national magazines and whose art and sensitivity fostered many charitable purposes. But his love of nature and deep understanding of humanity especially qualified him for this book which deals equally with two worlds. A long-time friend of the Kleins, he passed away in early 1988.